The History of VIDEO GAMING

James Roland

ReferencePoint Press

San Diego, CA

ReferencePoint Press®

Printed in the United States

For more information, contact:
ReferencePoint Press, Inc.
PO Box 27779
San Diego, CA 92198
www.ReferencePointPress.com

LIBRARY OF CONGRESS CATALOGING-IN-PUBLICATION DATA

Names: Roland, James author
Title: The history of video gaming / By James Roland.
Description: San Diego, CA : ReferencePoint Press, Inc, 2026. | Includes bibliographical references.
Identifiers: LCCN 2025032485 (print) | LCCN 2025032486 (ebook) | ISBN 9781678212421 library binding | ISBN 9781678212438 ebook
Subjects: LCSH: Video games--History--Juvenile literature | Video games industry--History--Juvenile literature
Classification: LCC GV1469.3 .R653 2026 (print) | LCC GV1469.3 (ebook) | DDC 794.8--dc23/eng/20250902
LC record available at https://lccn.loc.gov/2025032485
LC ebook record available at https://lccn.loc.gov/2025032486

CONTENTS

IMPORTANT EVENTS IN THE HISTORY OF VIDEO GAMING

1947
Americans Thomas T. Goldsmith Jr. and Estle Ray Mann file a patent for a cathode-ray tube amusement device, an early target game played on an oscilloscope.

1948
Englishmen Alan Turing and David Champernowne draft the algorithms for *Turochamp*, an early computer chess game that never was completed.

1958
William Higinbotham, a computer engineer with Brookhaven National Laboratory in New York, creates *Tennis for Two*, one of the first video games ever developed.

1962
Massachusetts Institute of Technology student Steve Russell invents *Spacewar!*, a computer-based, player-versus-player video game that was spread to other colleges with similar computer facilities.

1972
In California, Nolan Bushnell and Allan Alcorn at Atari develop an arcade table tennis game called *Pong*, which launched the golden age of arcade video games.

1980
Japanese company Namco releases *Pac-Man*, one of the most popular video games of all time that spawned a sequel (*Ms. Pac-Man*), a television cartoon, merchandise, and more.

1982
Disney releases the movie *Tron*, about a computer hacker who is pulled into a video game and must fight to return to the real world. A game based on the movie was a hit that year in US arcades, being named Coin-Operated Game of the Year by *Electronic Games* magazine.

1986
The Japanese video game corporation Nintendo releases the Nintendo Entertainment System (NES), revitalizing the home console market. The NES games *Super Mario Bros*. and *The Legend of Zelda* become massive hits worldwide.

1989
The Japanese company Sega releases the Genesis, its answer to the NES, and for the next several years the two consoles duel for video game supremacy.

1994
Concerns about video game violence prompt the creation of the Entertainment Software Ratings Board, a self-regulatory organization that begins rating games based on levels of violence and other controversial material.

1995
Japanese electronics giant Sony introduces the PlayStation console and follows it up in 2000 with the PlayStation 2, known as the PS2, still the all-time biggest-selling home game console.

1950 1960 1970 1980 1990

2001
Microsoft releases the Xbox, the tech company's first home console system.

2004
The Nintendo DS becomes a wildly popular handheld video game console, featuring games like *Mario Kart DS*.

2005
The Xbox 360 becomes a massive hit due to excellent graphics and seamless online play.

2006
The Nintendo Wii, with its unique graphics and motion-sensitive remotes, requires players to get up and move to control the game characters' actions in basketball, bowling, and other activity-based games.

2008
Blizzard's *World of Warcraft* surpasses 10 million subscribers, turning it into the most successful massively multiplayer online game of all time.

2009
Two years after its release, the Apple iPhone becomes a platform for millions of people to play games like *Angry Birds*, *Candy Crush*, and more.

2011
Mojang releases *Minecraft*, a building game that fosters creativity and teamwork. It becomes one of the world's most popular and successful video games of all time.

2016
Niantic's *Pokémon GO* becomes a worldwide fad and spurs interest in the development of video games featuring augmented reality.

2017
Nintendo releases the Switch, a hybrid game that can be played as a portable console or connected to a home console.

2020
Millions of people around the world turn to games such as Nintendo's *Animal Crossing: New Horizons*, Devolver Digital's *Fall Guys*, and Innersloth's *Among Us* to help them cope with the social isolation associated with the COVID-19 pandemic.

2025
A Minecraft Movie becomes one of the biggest box-office hits of the year, arriving in theaters just two years after the global smash *The Super Mario Bros. Movie*, which raked in more than $1 billion worldwide in 2023.

2000 2005 2010 2015 2020

Level Up: The Rise of Video Games

In the gymnasium of Windemere High School, a little southwest of Orlando, Florida, fans gathered for a state championship match like no other. The crowd roared with the introduction of each team. The athletes, feeling the tension, took their places. The match was on. "I was kind of nervous at the beginning being in front of the crowd," said Windemere junior John Bueno. "But once I got settled in, it was all good. When the game started, I was able to just let the nerves out."[1]

The game? *Rocket League*, an enormously popular video game in which players control cartoonish rocket-powered vehicles in order to knock an oversized soccer ball into their opponent's goal. The May 2024 Florida High School State Championship was the state's first in-person esport—short for "electronic sport," a competitive type of video gaming that is conducted in high schools, colleges, and professional tournaments around the world.

No longer just a means for kids to compete, esports have become a multibillion-dollar industry. Many professionals earn millions of dollars for their video game skills, and millions of viewers flock to esports tournaments both in person and online. Some colleges even give scholarships for students who play for the school's esports teams.

An Evolution in Gaming

Modern games like *Rocket League* are challenging to play. Some have movie-quality graphics and music, as well as clever characters and storylines. While some people choose to play them alone, others play cooperatively or against each other online. But video games were not always this dynamic. The earliest games were little more than blips of light that players could control—or try to control—and they could only be played on giant computers.

As computer technology advanced in the last half of the twentieth century and in the early decades of the twenty-first century, the quality and popularity of video games grew, too. Though today's video games can make it look, sound, and even sometimes feel like players are right in the middle of the action, the technology has not always mattered as much as the fun of the game itself. Games from the 1970s and 1980s, for example, with their simple, pixelated graphics and slow processing speeds (compared with today's lightning-fast video games), kept people entertained for hours at a time. And the current popularity of retro gaming featuring 8-bit heroes and spaceships proves pixels still have their place in the hearts of true gamers.

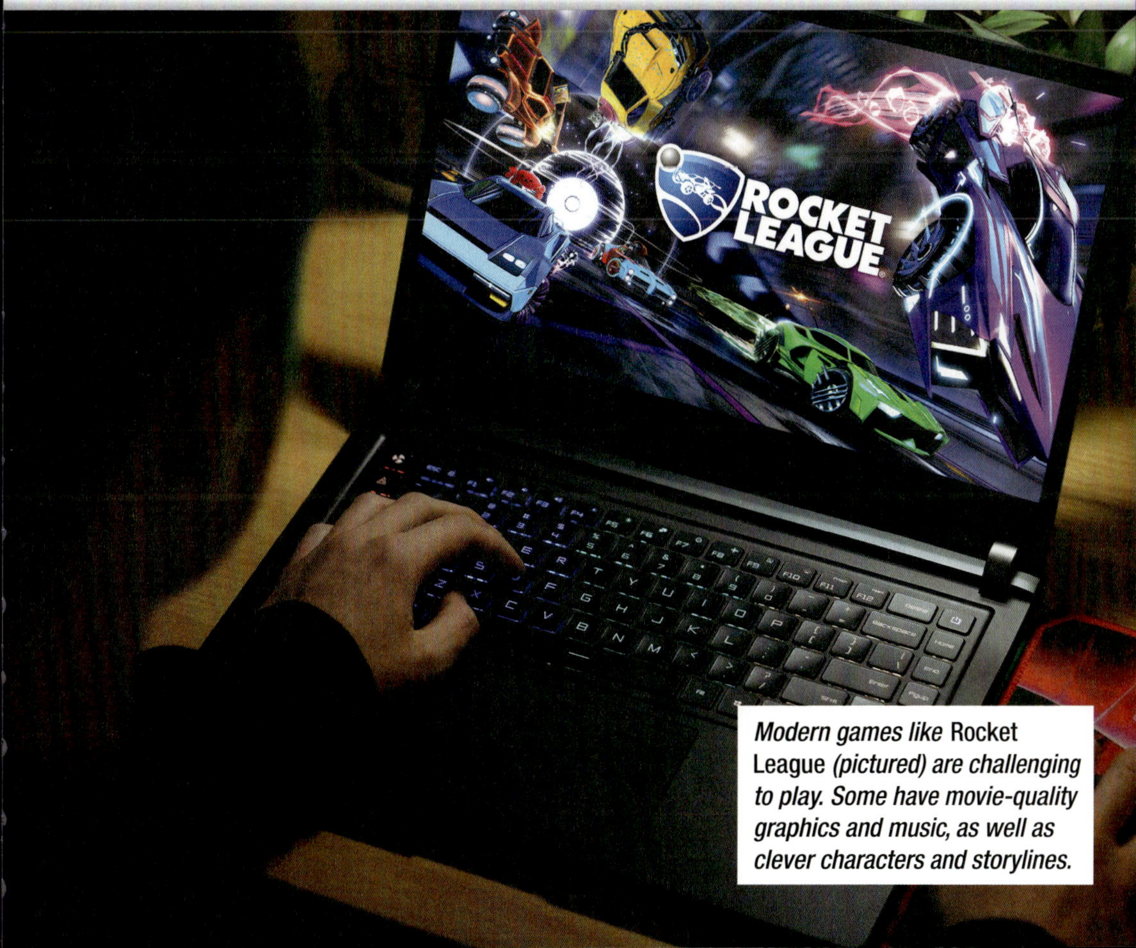

Modern games like Rocket League *(pictured) are challenging to play. Some have movie-quality graphics and music, as well as clever characters and storylines.*

Virtual Worlds, Real-World Impact

Video games have become more than just a way to race, fly spaceships, win shootouts, and have adventures in virtual worlds. They have continued to push advancements in the technology needed to play them. Improved graphics cards and faster processing speeds require computers, phones, and other devices to continually improve. Games have made their mark in pop culture and added countless expressions to modern language. Terms like *NPC*, *n00b*, and *power-up* are often heard well outside gaming environments.

And perhaps most importantly, video games have provided a means for people to connect. Whether players are seated on the same couch or interacting in the same online game despite being miles apart in real life, people find companionship and camaraderie in mastering the newest games. For instance, a 2024 study in the journal *Frontiers in Rehabilitation Sciences* found that individuals with spinal cord injuries, many of whom have a limited ability to get out and socialize, were able to develop and maintain social connections through online video games. And during the COVID-19 global lockdowns, video games proved to be valuable outlets for people around the world who otherwise felt isolated.

> **"Video games have been a fixture in American life and culture for generations."[2]**
>
> —Stanley Pierre-Louis, president and chief executive officer of the Entertainment Software Association

Friends and family members, separated by vast distances, can still stay in touch by playing *Fortnite*, *Minecraft*, *League of Legends*, *Brawl Stars*, and countless other games. "Video games have been a fixture in American life and culture for generations," says Stanley Pierre-Louis, president and chief executive officer (CEO) of the Entertainment Software Association. "Players of all ages, backgrounds and abilities are embracing the positivity that video games bring to their lives. While the games we play—and how we play them—evolves over time, what remains consistent is how video games enhance our lives in ways that inspire us and bring us closer together."[2]

Back at the Florida esports championships, the triumphant Windemere Wildcats embraced the future of video gaming, hoping other people would see the potential of games to bring people together while inspiring healthy competition. "This event is just the beginning," John Bueno says. "As time goes, the schools will start to see esports more and more like an actual sport—rather than just a game we play for fun."[3] Esports may be proving that video games are more than just pastimes. The skill, imagination, and technological innovation wrapped up in video games ensures that their impact will continue to be felt far beyond the screens on which they are played.

Press Start

Video games have roots in the earliest computers developed after World War II. Even as the first computer scientists were building machines to solve complex calculations and other problems, some of them were also finding ways to have fun with the new technology.

One of those early computer pioneers was Thomas T. Goldsmith Jr., who in 1947 submitted a patent for what he called the cathode-ray tube amusement device. Long before the development of digital flat-screen TVs, televisions were boxy appliances containing a cathode-ray tube (CRT) projector, which would emit beams of electrons through electrical coils and onto a glass screen. When he took a break from working on the first generation of postwar computers, Goldsmith built a CRT game that allowed the user to control beams of light to hit targets, which were just stickers placed on the screen. It was remarkably simple to play, but it was an early example of how engineers and scientists saw computers as more than problem solvers.

Goldsmith's machine used the analog technology of an oscilloscope—a device that measures electronic signals—and contained no computer circuitry. As a result, some video game historians do not consider it a true first in the field. Others, however, argue that Goldsmith's vision of the machine's commercial entertainment potential makes it a legitimate precursor to modern video games. Alex Magoun, a historian at the Institute of Electrical and Electronics Engineers in New Jersey, studied Goldsmith's creation. In an interview with *Popular Mechanics*, Magoun said that while the cathode-ray tube amusement device may seem like ancient technology these days, the same may be said of how every era of video games look to the generations that follow. "People may now look down at this technology from almost 75 years ago," he said, noting that the great-grandchildren of today's gamers may think the same of current video games. "Who can possibly imagine what games we're going to have in three generations?"[4]

> **"Who can possibly imagine what games we're going to have in three generations?"[4]**
>
> —Alex Magoun, historian at the Institute of Electrical and Electronics Engineers

Making Computers Fun

The early digital computers of the 1940s and 1950s took up entire rooms, were very expensive to build, and were designed to handle complex mathematical and physics computations. Only universities, a few large companies, and the military had the funds to build and house the giant mainframe computers, and therefore early computer development stemmed from these institutions.

Initially, computers were used for challenges, such as decrypting codes, simulating aircraft flight, forecasting weather patterns, and calculating things like the trajectory of missiles. Efforts to modernize military operations accelerated the pace of computer development in the United States, Great Britain, Germany, and

Long before the development of digital flat-screen TVs, televisions were boxy appliances containing a cathode-ray tube projector.

elsewhere. Businesses used early computers to help streamline tasks involving payroll and inventory. But as engineers designed new tasks for computing machines to test, they realized that computers offered unique opportunities for interactivity and could be used to play games.

In 1951, at the Festival of Britain's Exhibition of Science, engineers presented a computer that was built to play Nim, a traditional game of logic and strategy in which opponents alternate removing items from a few distinct piles until the last player is forced to take the single remaining item and thus wins (or sometimes loses) the game. Despite presenting an interactive challenge, the device was mainly designed to show off the computer's processing speed.

Then in 1958, at the Brookhaven National Laboratory in Upton, New York, physicist William Higinbotham introduced what is widely considered to be the first true video game. He called his creation *Tennis for Two*. It was played on a small oscilloscope that displayed the waveforms of electronic signals.

The oscilloscope screen showed a side view of a tennis court, a vertical line representing the net, and a dot representing the ball. The bright ball was the end of the oscilloscope waveform that arced across the court, and players used controllers to change the direction and angle of the wave to simulate hitting the ball across the net. The computer contained amplifiers that could sense whether the ball had crossed the net, but it was up to the players to keep score.

When the public got a chance to see and play *Tennis for Two* at the lab's annual open house, the line of curious wannabe gamers extended out the door. Years later, Higinbotham noted that allowing people to see how computers could be fun and have a place in everyday life was helpful in making technology more accessible to the general public. He wrote, "It might liven up the place to have a game that people could play, and which would convey the message that our scientific endeavors have relevance for society."[5]

Play On: Video Games Take Off

The development of new video games was slow throughout the 1960s. Early in the decade, a group of Massachusetts Institute of

Apple Grows from Atari

Steve Jobs and Steve Wozniak may be best known as the founders of Apple Computer in 1976. But just before they launched what would become one of the most influential tech companies in the world, Jobs and Wozniak were becoming friends at Atari, trying to streamline one of the video game company's early arcade hits, *Breakout*. Their goal was to reduce the number of computer chips needed to run the game. Most video games in the early 1970s required about one hundred chips, but Atari's lead engineers challenged Wozniak and Jobs to get the number below fifty. The pair managed to get *Breakout* to work with forty-six chips. Around this same time, Wozniak and Jobs were also tinkering with a personal home computer—a rare device in those days—that would eventually become the first Apple I computer. They even used some parts from the Atari workshops to finish their project in Jobs's garage. When their computer was completed, the young engineers offered it first to Atari. Seeing no future in home computers, Atari declined the offer. Jobs and Wozniak eventually found some investors, and before long Atari and Apple had both become two of the early giants of Silicon Valley.

Technology students, including Steve Russell, created a computer game called *Spacewar!* Inspired by the science-fiction novels they enjoyed and the growing popularity of science-fiction television shows and movies, *Spacewar!* was a dueling game in which each of two players controlled the movement and weapons of their own spaceship on-screen. They guided their ship and fired its lasers in hopes of destroying their opponent's ship first.

In an interview with *Smithsonian* magazine, Russell said he created *Spacewar!* to demonstrate how ships move in space. In the early 1960s, spaceflight and computers were still relatively new concepts, so he thought a game might be a fun and educational way to demystify complex science and engineering ideas for the average person. "*Spacewar!* was happily demonstrated as something understandable on a computer which was viewed as magic and incomprehensible,"[6] Russell says.

Spacewar! was designed and played on Digital Equipment Corporation PDP-1 computers, one of the earliest digital machines that had a CRT display and real-time output that provided immediate interactivity for users. Russell and his friends shared the code for the game freely with other computer students, who soon took the game to other universities around the country. It became extremely

> "*Pong* proved that there could be a market for a video game industry. It demonstrated that there could be companies and whole ecosystems based around video games."[7]
>
> —Tim Lapetino, author and pop culture historian

popular among students, but its use was limited to a handful of colleges with computers that were large enough to run the game.

To reach a wide audience of players, video games and their platforms needed to be more accessible and cheaper to mass-produce. While game designers tinkered with standalone video game machines for arcades in the late 1960s and early 1970s, a breakthrough finally occurred when a small Northern California company called Atari released *Pong* in 1972. The game, a somewhat more sophisticated version of *Tennis for Two*, was an instant hit, and *Pong* arcade machines began to appear in bars and public amusement centers.

Within just a few years, *Pong* and other video games were crowding out traditional pinball machines in arcades around the world. "*Pong* proved that there could be a market for a video game industry," author and pop culture historian Tim Lapetino told *SFGate* in 2023. "It demonstrated that there could be companies and whole ecosystems based around video games."[7] As proof, just ten years after the release of *Pong*, *The New York Times* in 1982 cited Atari's $2 billion in sales and called it "probably the fastest growing company in the nation."[8]

With the popularity of* Pong *(pictured) soaring in the 1970s, game companies around the world started churning out new video games.

Golden Age of Arcades

Before the 1970s, arcades were mainly populated by pinball machines, pool tables, and other games. With the popularity of *Pong* soaring, game companies around the world started churning out new video games.

Taito, a Japanese toy and game company, had some early successes, such as *Speed Race*, which featured a steering wheel controller, and *Western Gun*, a shooter game that shaped its controllers like revolver handles. In 1976 Sega, another Japanese company, became a producer of popular games, such as *Moto-Cross*, which featured haptic sensors that allowed players to feel the handlebar controllers vibrate during collisions, and the boxing-themed *Heavyweight Champ* that some consider the first hand-to-hand fighting game.

But the golden age of arcade video games really began in 1978, when Taito released *Space Invaders*, first in Japan and then the rest of the world. By today's standards, *Space Invaders* is a low-tech game. Players control a laser cannon at the bottom of the screen and attempt to shoot rows of descending alien ships before they reach the bottom.

As simple as it was, *Space Invaders* was nevertheless among the most influential video games of all time. It was so popular in its initial release that arcades became the new hot spots for young people. As Jonathan Ackley, a video game historian and professional game designer who cocreated the video game *The Curse of Monkey Island*, explained in a 2024 interview on the website GamesBeat:

> **"*Space Invaders* reshaped the arcade. When it came out, it dominated. Pinball machines were once the backbone of the arcade. After *Space Invaders*, it was all video games."[9]**
>
> —Jonathan Ackley, video game historian and professional game designer

> *Space Invaders* reshaped the arcade. When it came out, it dominated. Pinball machines were once the backbone of the arcade. After *Space Invaders*, it was all video games. When Taito launched the game in 1978, it became so

popular that it sucked up so many 100-yen coins, that Japan endured a coin shortage. The Japanese mint had to triple production of the coin to meet demand. Then *Space Invaders* conquered America.[9]

Space Invaders spawned the popularity of space-battle games and was one of the first video games in which the computer enemy fired back at the player. *Space Invaders* also popularized the idea of a "high score," as the game saved the scores of its top players. This also enticed more people to flock to arcades. Soon after *Space Invaders* made its mark, similar games filled the corners of arcades around the world. They included *Defender*, *Galaga*, and the game that would soon top *Space Invaders* as Atari's most successful game, *Asteroids*.

Pac-Man Fever

Most space-battle games were marketed to teenage boys and young men. Game designers soon realized, however, that they could reach a much wider audience if they developed a greater variety of games that would appeal to everyone. As a result, the

Pac-Man's popularity inspired sequels, including Ms. Pac-Man, a hit pop song called "Pac-Man Fever," and an animated television series.

Classic Arcade Games Are Now Collectors' Items

When arcade owners started buying games like *Space Invaders* and *Pac-Man* in the 1970s and 1980s, they paid anywhere from $1,500 to $3,000 for each machine. It was a good investment, since a popular game could bring in a few hundred dollars—all in quarters or tokens—per week. But when the golden age of the arcade came to an end and arcades started closing, those well-used machines were often sold at auction or simply thrown out. However, by the end of the 1990s and early 2000s, classic arcade games had become collectors' items. YouTube videos, online forums, and other social media continue to bring collectors and sellers together. While some classic arcade games go for as little as a few hundred dollars, some collectors are willing to spend $10,000 or more for rare games in good condition. But not all collectors are hobbyists. Some people, like Bashi Alee, who opened the Quarter Drop Arcade in Cottage Grove, Oregon, in 2025, have been hunting for old arcade games to stock new arcades. "This really is a love letter to the true, authentic, retro arcade experience," Alee told *Eugene Weekly*.

Quoted in Samantha Sobel, "Pinball Wizards," *Eugene (OR) Weekly*, March 13, 2025. https://eugeneweekly.com.

1980s saw the rise of video games based on cartoonish characters and situations that did not involve combat. The first big hit in this new generation was *Pac-Man*, released by the Japanese entertainment corporation Namco in 1980. The game, featuring a round character who gobbles up dots for points while being chased through a maze by colorful ghosts with names like Blinky and Clyde, became an international phenomenon and remains one of the best-selling games of all time. *Pac-Man* creator Toru Iwatani was a young game designer in the late 1970s when he set out to design a game that was less about fighting and more about silliness and fun. He told CNN in 2020, "When I started drafting up this project in the late 1970s, the arcades were filled with violent games all about killing aliens. They were gloomy places where only boys went to hang out. What I wanted to do was make arcades into livelier places that women and couples might enjoy visiting, so I thought it best to design a game with women in mind."[10]

Beyond the Arcade

Pac-Man's popularity inspired sequels, including *Ms. Pac-Man*, a hit pop song called "Pac-Man Fever," an animated television series, and merchandise ranging from breakfast cereals and popsicles to

T-shirts and jewelry. It proved the broader marketability of video games and their immediate impact on pop culture. *Pac-Man* also led the way for a new generation of video games. *Donkey Kong*, *Dig Dug*, *Centipede*, *Frogger*, *Q*bert*, *Super Mario*, and other whimsical games attracted a wider range of gamers looking for more than space battles and shootouts. And arcades held sway as the popular hangouts for youth culture through the mid-1980s.

However, as the popularity of video games grew, these arcade-style machines could be found in restaurants, movie theater lobbies, bowling alleys, convenience stores, gas stations, supermarkets, and even doctor and dentist offices. Restaurant chains such as ShowBiz Pizza and Chuck E. Cheese were developed specifically to draw in the arcade crowd.

Dedicated arcades struggled to stay lucrative when players could enjoy video games in the host of other venues. A new type of game, known as beat 'em up or brawler games, renewed interest in arcades for a brief time. Popular games included *Kung-Fu Master*, *Final Fight*, and *Teenage Mutant Ninja Turtles*. The two-player fighting games were simple to learn but difficult to master, which kept players coming back for more action. But even these games could be set up anywhere, and eventually many arcades had to shutter their storefronts.

Chris Trimper, whose family owns the modern video arcade Marty's Playland in Ocean City, Maryland, remembers every detail of the arcades of his summer vacations long ago. "There was something special about once or twice a summer getting to go to the arcade and play pinball and *Pac-Man*," he told ABC News. But Trimper's attempt to keep the arcade alive in the twenty-first century is daunting. Noting that modern economics do not favor the classic arcade model, he states. "It's hard to make money a quarter at a time."[11]

While the ubiquity of arcade games was partly responsible for the demise of many arcades, another factor ensured that players did not have to gather at commercial businesses to enjoy the latest games. They could play them at home. By the late 1970s and early 1980s, avid gamers could own their own video game consoles. A whole new era of video games was dawning.

Video Games Find a New Home

While millions of video game fans patiently waited with quarters in hand for a chance to play the newest games at the local arcade in the 1970s and 1980s, game manufacturers realized there was a massive audience of potential players sitting at home watching TV. In those days nearly every American home had a television. And with the right technology and game design, all those televisions could easily become video game monitors. Gamers could be little kids, parents, or grandparents—folks who might be less likely to hang out in an arcade, waiting in line for a chance to play *Space Invaders*.

All that was needed was for someone to develop a way to play computer games on a television. One of the most influential home video game pioneers was Ralph Baer, an electrical engineer working for Sanders Associates in New Hampshire in the late 1960s. With the help of a couple of other engineers, Baer developed what is considered one of the first home video game systems. It was called the Brown Box because it looked like a wooden box, and it was easily attached to standard television sets. The console included games like Ping-Pong, soccer, target shooting, checkers, and golf.

Sanders eventually licensed Baer's product to the television manufacturer Magnavox, which sold the device as the Magnavox Odyssey beginning in 1972. The gaming system, which originally sold for $99 (the equivalent of about $750 in 2025), was not a big hit. Its price and the fact that it was available only for use with Magnavox TVs limited its appeal. Magnavox discontinued the game console in 1975.

Adding to the Odyssey's troubles was a dispute over the rights to its *Table Tennis* game, which looked and played a lot like the wildly popular arcade game *Pong*. A long legal battle took place between Baer and Nolan Bushnell, who had developed an arcade version of *Pong* along with computer engineer Allan Alcorn for Atari before the Odyssey hit the shelves.

Despite the poor performance of the Magnavox Odyssey, Atari saw the potential of the arcade game *Pong* as a home video game. Just in time for Christmas 1975, Atari released a home version, and it became one of the biggest hits of the holiday season. Capitalizing on its success, Atari introduced its 2600 gaming console in 1977 along with dozens of new games. The development of a cartridge-based gaming console that could play many different games, which was known then as a video computer system (VCS), meant there was conceivably no limit to the number and variety of video games that could be played at home. "*Pong* was important, but I think the VCS . . . was much more impactful,"[12] Bushnell said in a 2022 interview with AARP.

> "*Pong* was important, but I think the VCS [the cartridge-based console] . . . was much more impactful."[12]
>
> —Nolan Bushnell, developer of the arcade version of *Pong*

Over the next fifteen years, Atari sold about 30 million home consoles. During the early years of the home video game revolution, other companies got in on the action. The competition not only put more games and home consoles on store shelves, it also pushed game designers to keep improving graphics, processing speed, and other game features.

The 1980s Boom

Tech companies rushed their home video game consoles onto the market throughout the 1980s. The sheer volume of gaming systems and the poor quality of many of them led to a brief crash in home system popularity in 1983. At that point, the Atari 2600 (and later the upgraded 5200) console and American toy maker Mattel's Intellivision console were the biggest sellers, but there was some concern that home video games were a fad that might be dying out.

Then in 1985, a Japanese company called Nintendo released the Nintendo Entertainment System (NES) in North America, and

In 1985, a Japanese company called Nintendo released the Nintendo Entertainment System. The breakout hit among the seventeen initial games was Super Mario Bros.

the longevity of the home video game industry was assured. The breakout hit among the seventeen initial NES games was *Super Mario Bros.*, an extension of the 1983 arcade hit *Mario Bros.* Nintendo's string of hits continued with *The Legend of Zelda* (1986), *Punch-Out!!* (1987), and *DuckTales* (1989).

It was not just the number of games Nintendo introduced every year that made the NES so popular. For example, the NES game controller was the first to feature the cross-style D-pad (for direction), which is standard on most controllers today. And for the first time, players could save their game on a console.

The Early 1990s Console Competition

Nintendo's NES was clearly the king of the home video game world heading into the 1990s, but two other gaming systems were coming for the crown. The first was Sega's Genesis and its speedy little mascot, Sonic the Hedgehog. Besides Sonic's signature game, Sega also introduced a lot of sports games, including the first edition of *Madden NFL*, which would go on to become one of the most popular sports video game franchises, with annual releases that continue to this day.

In the battle for home video game supremacy, Sega made the strategic decision to market games primarily toward teens and young adults. Its games included rock music soundtracks and fast characters like Sonic in order to appear as a cooler alternative to Nintendo. Sega also employed celebrities like National Football League quarterback Joe Montana in commercials for its games. Al Nilsen, who was Sega of America's director of marketing in the 1990s, acknowledged that most of the kids playing Nintendo were twelve and under and that Sega probably could not compete for that group. He also realized that because Sega had some classic arcade game titles, like *Golden Axe* and *Space Harrier*, it could lead the way in re-creating the arcade experience in home video games. The company soon released other popular arcade games, such as *Mortal Kombat* and *Street Fighter*. Nilsen told *The Guardian* in 2019, "I looked at who was playing in the arcades—and this was back in the day, when they were on every street corner—and it wasn't six to 12-year-old boys, it was teenagers and young adults. They went there be-

Violent Games Lead to Ratings and Research

There has long been concern among parents, psychologists, and others that young people who play violent video games are more likely to act violently or aggressively in real life. In the 1990s, when popular games like *Mortal Kombat* started featuring realistic violence, the public outcry grew too loud to ignore. To avoid potential government censorship, gaming companies formed the Entertainment Software Rating Board in 1994. The regulatory organization assigned age and content ratings based on a game's violence, sexual content, drug references, language, and other potentially problematic elements. Even with ratings attached to each game, worries about violent content did not go away. In 2000 the *Journal of Personality and Social Psychology* published two studies suggesting that violent video games may increase a person's aggressive thoughts and behaviors. Other studies have found that video game violence may twist a player's sense of right and wrong or dampen sympathy toward others. However, plenty of research has shown such changes are minor and tend to affect a small percentage of players—often those who may already have anger issues. While concerns about video game violence continue, researchers are still working to better understand how games might affect real-world behavior.

cause that's where the best games were."[13] Sega hoped to pull in that audience.

> "I looked at who was playing in the arcades . . . and it wasn't six to 12-year-old boys, it was teenagers and young adults. They went there because that's where the best games were."[13]
>
> —Al Nilsen, Sega of America's director of marketing in the 1990s

Despite strong marketing, the Sega Genesis system was a short-lived phenomenon. By the end of the 1990s, Sega had discontinued its Genesis consoles, though it has released different versions of the system through the years and licensed the Genesis name to other video game companies to make Genesis-like consoles and games. But in its relatively short heyday, Sega changed the video game industry by making games "cool" and expanding the population of gamers to include teens and adults. In an essay on the twenty-fifth anniversary of Sega Genesis, Adrian Sandoval, a professional game developer who also teaches video game design and history at Drexel University, wrote:

> If the Atari generation introduced video games as a short-lived '70s fad—the electronic equivalent of a Pet Rock—and the NES generation established it into an enduring obsession for the young, Sega's Genesis began pushing the medium toward something resembling its contemporary form. Genesis was heavy on violence, on sports, and on image: Fundamental components of the engine that helps fuel today's console industry.[14]

The New Graphics Revolution

While the first half of 1990s belonged to Nintendo and Sega, the second half ushered in the most successful home video game system of all time. When introduced in Japan in 1994 and elsewhere a year later, the Sony PlayStation sold out immediately. In the United States alone, one hundred thousand units were purchased within two days of launch.

One of the main features that set PlayStation apart from NES and Sega Genesis was its 3-D graphics. Up to that point,

One of the main features that set PlayStation apart from NES and Sega Genesis was its 3-D graphics. Up to that point, most video games in the arcade and at home used 2-D imagery.

most video games in the arcade and at home used 2-D imagery: sometimes flashy but ultimately flat. PlayStation games, however, invited players into the action as never before. The 3-D capability was especially exciting for role-playing adventure games, such as *Final Fantasy* and *Dragon Quest*. The next-level graphics also helped make the fast-paced racing game *Gran Turismo* one of PlayStation's all-time biggest sellers. In an article on the entertainment website IGN about the thirtieth anniversary of the first PlayStation, Shawn Layden, former president and CEO of Sony Interactive Entertainment America, recalled how quickly Sony's games and console captured the imagination of gamers. He said, "No matter your gaming tastes, there was something for you on PlayStation. Sony's advancements in both technology and business strategy had pushed the games industry into a vibrant and varied new place. By 1999, the company had claimed an astonishing 60% of the American video game market."[15]

"No matter your gaming tastes, there was something for you on PlayStation."[15]

—Shawn Layden, former president and CEO of Sony Interactive Entertainment America

The 3-D quality and the overall gaming experience improved dramatically with PlayStation 2 (often referred to simply as PS2), which came out in 2000. The PS2 is still the best-selling game console of all time, with more than 160 million units sold globally. Since then, Sony has released newer generation PlayStation consoles with slicker graphics, faster processing speeds, and other updated features. Since 1994 more than 500 million PlayStation consoles have been sold worldwide, according to the video game news site VGChartz, making it the best-selling home video game system of all time.

A New Millennium of Home Video Games

Despite Sony's dominance in the early 2000s, the PlayStation's rivals were not ready to step back just yet. And one major tech company also decided to get in the game just as the twenty-first century arrived.

In 2001 Microsoft introduced the Xbox, the first video game console with a built-in hard drive, which made it better than its competitors at saving games and storing both player data and downloaded content. The Xbox also allowed for expansion cards and external SSDs (portable storage devices) to increase storage and facilitate larger game libraries. Xbox also made its mark by having exclusive games, such as the commercially successful and critically acclaimed *Halo: Combat Evolved*.

World Video Game Hall of Fame

Not far from Lake Ontario in the northern reaches of New York state lies one of the greatest video game collections in the world. Housed in the Strong National Museum of Play in Rochester is the World Video Game Hall of Fame. Every year, museum officials welcome a new "class" of electronic games of all kinds—arcade, console, handheld, mobile, and computer—into the hall of fame. The games are chosen because of their popularity or their influence on the gaming industry, pop culture, or society in general. The first class, chosen in 2015, included *Pac-Man*, *Doom*, *Tetris*, *World of Warcraft*, *Super Mario Bros.*, and of course, *Pong*, the one that started it all. Other inductees include classics such as *Dance Dance Revolution*, *The Oregon Trail*, and *The Last of Us*. The hall of fame offers visitors both history and fun, with interactive displays and opportunities to play some of the all-time great games. There are also exhibits that illustrate the evolution of video games. The Strong National Museum of Play also features the National Toy Hall of Fame and other exhibitions.

The Xbox was not Microsoft's first venture into the video game world. The company pioneered personal computer (PC) gaming as far back as 1982 with its *Microsoft Flight Simulator* game. One of its biggest hits arrived in 1997 with *Age of Empires*, a world-building and research-management strategy game that spawned several sequels and set the stage for hugely popular PC games like *World of Warcraft* and *Minecraft* that would arrive a few years later.

In the 1990s Microsoft saw console-based games booming and was not content to just keep making PC-based games. But the company knew that it had to offer gamers something PlayStation did not have at the time. That feature was called Xbox Live (now known as the Xbox network), and it allowed players to compete and download content online. Although the PS2 permitted online play, it required a separate network adapter to connect to the internet. The Xbox's networking capability was built into the console.

The smooth, high-speed internet capabilities of the Xbox set it apart from other gaming systems that offered online options. Many of those either used slower dial-up connections or were simply less consistent than the broadband connectivity of the Xbox. "With broadband gaming, you could just have a better quality game experience, and it really changed everything,"[16] IGN executive editor Ryan McCaffrey told ABC News in a story about Xbox's twentieth anniversary in 2021.

In 2006, five years after the Xbox hit store shelves, Nintendo answered with the Wii. Nintendo hoped that the Wii's family-friendly games and graphics would appeal to children and adults alike. For a while, Nintendo's gamble paid off. Wii controllers required users to move around, swinging their arms to hit virtual tennis balls, for example, or simulate activities like shooting a basketball or swinging a golf club—quite a different gaming experience than that offered by its competitors. *Wii Sports Resort*, which compiled twelve sports games, became a cultural phenomenon. Schools used the game for rainy-day physical education classes, and retirement centers got older adults up and moving with Wii bowling tournaments.

Wii's family-friendly games and graphics appealed to children and adults alike. Some Wii controllers allowed users to do things like move around, swinging their arms to hit virtual tennis balls, for example.

But by 2010 sales of the Wii had started to slide. Nintendo responded with systems that could play more advanced games, such as the Wii U and the Wii Mini, but within a few years, Nintendo discontinued the Wii and its many games and online services. However, the company was set to release a new gaming option that would reestablish its dominance in the video game world. The Nintendo Switch, released in 2017, was a hybrid of handheld and home console systems. More than fifty years into their rapidly evolving and ever-changing landscape, video games were still a dominant form of entertainment.

CHAPTER THREE

Games in the Palm of Your Hand

Despite their popularity, arcade games and home video games had one shared drawback. They required players to remain in one place—at the arcade or at home in front of the television. Sensing the potential of portable video games, in the mid-1970s toy and game companies like Mattel, Coleco, and Milton Bradley began introducing handheld electronic game devices and new games to be played on them.

Mattel started things off with a simple racing game called *Auto Race*. Players guided their "cars," which were just blips of light, from the bottom of the screen to the top, swerving to avoid other cars. A collision sent the player's car to the bottom of the screen to start over. Mattel then produced several similar sports-themed handheld games, all based on moving a blip of light. The football, baseball, basketball, and hockey games all sold well and fueled the market for more handheld video games. The games were relatively inexpensive, simple to play, and portable. They fit neatly into a school backpack, and before long the beeps of handheld games resounded throughout school buses everywhere.

The idea for the games originated when a couple of product engineers at Mattel proposed converting a handheld calculator into a game. Their concept was among several that Mattel pitched to Rockwell International, an Anaheim, California–based tech company. A young Rockwell circuit designer named Mark Lesser was immediately intrigued by the calculator-game proposal. "I looked at that and my eyes popped—not because I realized it was going to be a big thing, but because I love games," he told *Popular Mechan-*

ics. "I had always been a pinball player, any sort of electronic or arcade game. I just loved that kind of stuff, so I grabbed it and went with it."[17]

Those early handheld devices played just one game, but in 1979 Milton Bradley, best known as the company responsible for board games such as Candy Land and Battleship, released Microvision, the first handheld console with interchangeable game cartridges. Although its graphics and games were simple, Microvision set the stage for much more sophisticated portable games to come. At around that same time, Nintendo introduced its Game & Watch series. Like Mattel's single-game options, Game & Watch consisted of self-contained games, but they featured some innovations that would become staples of future game controllers. Among them was the D-pad, short for "directional pad." The feature was a cross-shaped button that allowed players to use a thumb to move characters or other items in the game up or down and right or left.

In the 1980s, Nintendo introduced its Game & Watch series. It featured some innovations that would become staples of future game controllers.

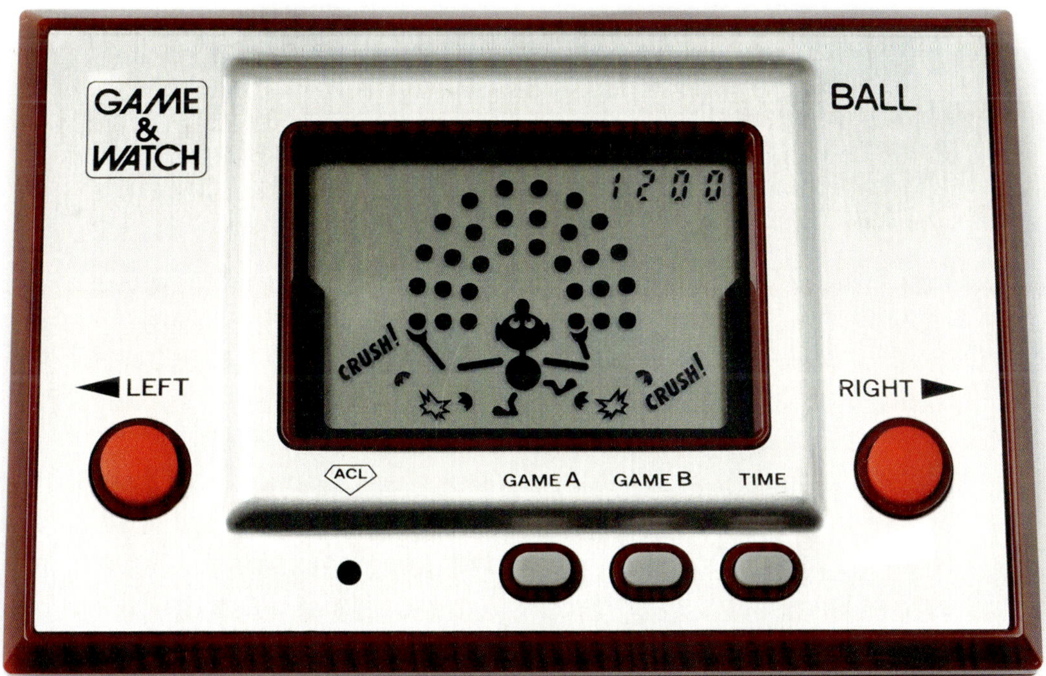

Game Boy Changes the Game

As home video games were getting more sophisticated, gamers' appetite for cooler handheld platforms was growing. Nintendo again responded with the Game Boy, which made its North American debut on July 31, 1989. That day, forty thousand units were sold. By the end of the summer, 1 million more Game Boys had been purchased. "Game Boy was not the first handheld gaming system, but it was certainly the most popular,"[18] says Drew Robarge, a museum specialist at the National Museum of American History in Washington, DC, where a first-generation Game Boy is on display alongside early cell phones and other items that had big impacts on the culture.

> **"Game Boy was not the first handheld gaming system, but it was certainly the most popular."[18]**
>
> —Drew Robarge, specialist at the National Museum of American History in Washington, DC

Unlike the single-game units, such as Mattel's early portable hits, the Game Boy was a handheld console that could play many different types of games. Players could easily swap out game cartridges just like they could with their home consoles. Early Game Boy hits included *Super Mario Land* and *Tetris*. Until 1989, *Tetris* was a somewhat popular arcade game, but Nintendo included the game with the Game Boy console itself, and before long millions of people were hooked. "Nintendo saw *Tetris* and realized it was the killer app for the Game Boy," Robarge says. "It's perfect for traveling, you can play for five minutes or an hour and still be satisfied. Game Boy definitely helped *Tetris* rise to the top."[19]

Game Boy was not the only handheld hit of 1989. Atari, still a force in the home video game world, released its handheld console called Lynx that same year. The graphics and game playing of the 16-bit Lynx system were superior to the Game Boy's 8-bit consoles. Though initially popular, the Lynx never really had a chance. Atari released seventy-one games for the Lynx, while Nintendo produced almost eleven hundred games for the Game Boy. Atari soon followed the Lynx with the Jaguar handheld console, but it never made much of a splash among gamers. It would

The Risks of Too Much Gaming

Too much time spent playing video games can interfere with school, work, sleep, and doing other things that are important or just fun in other ways. And some mental health experts suggest that it is possible to become addicted to playing video games. Video game addiction (VGA), also called gaming disorder, is usually defined as compulsive game playing that interferes with people's ability to function in various other aspects of their lives over an extended period. There is some debate about whether VGA should be considered a mental health disorder on the same level as depression or obsessive-compulsive disorder, for example, but the American Psychiatric Association has called for further study on the subject. Signs of VGA include giving up other activities that were once enjoyable, encountering sleep problems, experiencing mood changes, lying to others about time spent playing video games, spending a lot of time thinking about games, and feeling a need to spend more time playing. Talking with a parent or doctor about such issues may be helpful. There are also screening tests that can help diagnose a possible gaming disorder.

be the last new video game system produced by Atari—the company that kicked off the video game revolution with *Pong*—before dropping out of the hardware market in 1996.

Despite Atari's withdrawal, the Game Boy still faced competition. Its biggest rival was the Game Gear, a handheld system made by Sega. While many initial Game Boy games offered only black-and-white graphics, the Game Gear sought to capture audiences with full-color games. But the Game Boy with its monochrome graphics required less processing than the backlit LCD screen of the Game Gear. This proved to be an advantage for Nintendo. While the Game Gear required six AA batteries and tended to use up those batteries relatively quickly, the Game Boy needed only four AA batteries for its slower processor, and thus gamers could play much longer. The Game Gear also released fewer than half of the games that were available for the Game Boy. And while Nintendo continued to make newer, better versions of the Game Boy, including the Game Boy Color and Game Boy Advance, Sega made few improvements to the Game Gear over time. Sega eventually bowed to the Game Boy's success and discontinued the Game Gear in 1997.

The Game Boy rode a wave of unprecedented success, selling more than 118 million units by the time Nintendo discontinued it in 2003. At that time, the Game Boy was the biggest-selling handheld video game console of all time. But Nintendo fans did not have to wait long. The next big thing was about to hit store shelves around the world.

Games Take Another Leap

Though their speed, graphics, and available games differed, much of the technology in handheld video game units was similar across brands. But the Nintendo DS changed the nature of handheld games forever. *DS* stood for both "Dual Screen" and "Developers' System," though it was the two screens on the portable, foldable console that largely set it apart from its competitors.

One of those screens was also a touch screen, which at the time was a novelty in handheld games. On the game enthusiast website Nintendo Life, writer Damien McFerran noted that "DS was the first encounter many people had with touch-based tech, and it left an indelible impression."[20]

"DS was the first encounter many people had with touch-based tech, and it left an indelible impression."[20]

—Damien McFerran, writer for Nintendo Life

Nintendo DS was also notable because it was designed to connect to the internet, which was still a relatively new feature for handheld or console video game systems. The ability for DS players to compete against other players online in *Pokémon Dash*, *Super Mario*, *Rayman*, *Madden NFL*, and dozens of other games was a whole new way to enjoy what previously had been a pretty solitary gaming experience.

Nintendo consistently put out new, upgraded versions of the DS system, such as Nintendo 3DS and Nintendo DS Lite. Together, all Nintendo DS models combined for more than 154 million units sold, far surpassing the Game Boy. The DS also expanded the market for handheld games. For a long time, the majority of video game players were male, but the DS attracted many more female gamers. In 2006 about half of all DS players were female, and the majority of players of one of the most popular DS games—the real-time puppy simulation game *Nintendogs*—were girls.

Despite its popularity, Nintendo discontinued the DS family of devices in 2014. At that time, the company was developing the Nintendo Switch, the most versatile video console yet developed. The handheld unit could be used on its own, like the DS, but it could also be connected to a home television and function similar to a console. The Switch could also be played by one player or by two, simply by removing the two small controllers on either side of the device. The Switch also allowed for even faster, smoother, high-speed online gaming than was available on any DS model. The Switch proved an instant success upon its launch in March 2017, selling nearly 15 million units by December. However, the market for portable video gaming was changing in the mid-2010s, and though the Switch would remain popular—and would evolve into the Switch 2 in 2025—another commonplace technology had already swiftly transformed the way many people accessed and played games.

Smartphones Become Game Consoles

The arrival of smartphones in the early 2000s unleashed a tidal wave of new games and gaming options. Early Nokia cell phones—those without the advanced computing capabilities of today's smartphones—could play some simple preloaded games

The real birth of mobile games coincided with the introduction of the iPhone in 2007. One of the first popular smartphone games included Clash of Clans *(pictured).*

when they first appeared on the scene in the 1990s. But the real birth of mobile games coincided with the introduction of the iPhone in 2007 and Apple's App Store in 2008. Like today's App Store, the original version offered apps related to news, shopping, and of course, plenty of games.

Games represent the single biggest category of apps in Apple's App Store (about 11.86 percent of the total number of available apps). Games are also the most sought-after apps in the Google Play Store. Some of the first popular smartphone games included *Candy Crush*, *Angry Birds*, *Clash of Clans*, *Pokémon GO*, and *Words with Friends*. As smartphone graphics, memory, and processing speeds have improved, games once reserved for PCs and consoles—like *Call of Duty* and *Among Us*—have developed huge player bases on cell phone platforms.

It is more than just improved technology that has boosted smartphone (also known as mobile) gaming. However, it is worth noting that the use of smartphones as game consoles has led to improvements in various aspects of the phones themselves. The addition of more features in games has spurred the demand for greater storage options to accommodate larger game files and updates. Smartphone manufacturers have responded with

Free-to-Play Games? Not Always

Fortnite is free to download and play. The same is true for countless other games players load onto their mobile devices or their handheld or home consoles. But as with so many free things in life, there is a catch. It is called a microtransaction. In many games, for a fee—often starting at around ninety-nine cents but sometimes costing much more—players can purchase items or upgrades to give their game character advantages in the game. This type of microtransaction is sometimes referred to sarcastically as "pay-to-win." In many games, including *Fortnite*, players also can buy "skins," which simply change the looks of characters, weapons, or vehicles, rather than afford the characters any advantages in the game. Game developers defend microtransactions as a way to make some money from their free games, noting that players are not required to buy anything. These purchases are always optional. But critics of microtransactions say the practice may be inappropriate, especially when children feel pressured to spend money to enjoy or have a chance of winning a supposedly "free" game. In recent years, lawmakers around the world have started to pass laws and investigate ways to regulate microtransactions.

One of the first popular smartphone games was Pokémon GO *(pictured). Games once reserved for PCs and consoles developed huge player bases on smartphone platforms.*

increased built-in storage capacities. Manufacturers are also focusing more on making the screens bigger without necessarily increasing the size of the phones themselves.

Another major factor is the sheer volume of new games that are available year after year. Tech journalist Chris Lakewoods, writing for TechBullion, noted that developing and releasing new games takes much less time and effort for mobile devices than it does for home consoles. In 2024 he wrote, "Mobile games tend to have shorter testing cycles, thanks to their simpler gameplay mechanics and smaller scale. Mobile developers can quickly identify bugs, release patches, and test across a limited range of devices. Since mobile games often rely on user feedback, frequent updates are common, allowing developers to improve or add features post-launch."[21]

Mobile games also continue to flourish because billions of people around the world have smartphones. Casual gamers may not be interested in purchasing a separate portable console when the phone they already have can let them play a seemingly endless array of solo games or games with others who are miles away.

And yet, despite some advantages, smartphone gaming has not wiped out the competition from the Switch and other handheld game consoles. In a 2025 article on the website How-to Geek, writer Sydney Butler explains that while people may not mind if their handheld console runs out of battery and needs to be recharged, no one wants to see their phone battery power get too low or run out altogether. He also notes that after a phone's operating system is updated, mobile games can sometimes be hard to play (or even impossible to play) without deleting them and downloading them again. That problem does not exist with handheld consoles. One other advantage handheld systems have over their mobile counterparts is that there are relatively few high-quality premium games available for smartphones compared with home or portable consoles. "This means that modern handhelds have carved out a niche for themselves that it seems mobile devices simply can't fill, and so they can exist side-by-side,"[22] Butler wrote.

"Modern handhelds have carved out a niche for themselves that it seems mobile devices simply can't fill, and so they can exist side-by-side."[22]

—Sydney Butler, writer for How-to Geek

Even though portable and mobile systems meant the games got smaller, the popularity of games on the go is only growing. And ongoing improvements in technology are only making those handheld games more exciting and more fun to play.

CHAPTER FOUR

More than Just a Game

Some of the highest-grossing movies of the 2020s include *Sonic the Hedgehog*, *Sonic the Hedgehog 2*, *Sonic the Hedgehog 3*, *The Super Mario Bros. Movie*, and *A Minecraft Movie*. Each of them raked in more than $300 million in ticket sales worldwide, and a couple of them cleared more than $1 billion at the box office. As their titles indicate, they are all based on popular video games.

While not all video game adaptations are smash hits, film producers know that plenty of people familiar with a game may be willing to check out a related movie with familiar characters and game imagery. This is not a new phenomenon, however. In fact, there was a big-budget *Super Mario Bros.* movie released in 1993, though it was something of a box office bomb. And before that, in 1982 Disney released a film called *Tron*, in which a computer hacker is pulled into a video game and must win a series of fights and contests to survive and return to the real world. A video game based on some of the movie's big action sequences became a hit at arcades that same year.

But movies are not the only ways video games have powered their way into popular culture. TV shows, popular music, fashion, and even everyday language reflect the popularity of video gaming. And video games—particularly their combination of graphics, storytelling, and soundtracks—are finally being taken seriously as art. In 2022, New York's Museum of Modern Art mounted an exhibition called *Never Alone*, which featured dozens of video games from the past fifty years.

From Loading Screens to Big and Small Screens

Adapting video games into movies and TV series has always made sense. The titles and characters are well known, and the

Some of the highest-grossing movies of the 2020s include Sonic the Hedgehog *(pictured). The movie was based on a popular video game.*

familiar world of the games can be made more spectacular and exciting with big budgets and often big stars. But not every adaptation is successful. For every *Super Mario Bros. Movie* and *A Minecraft Movie* that are big hits, there are films like *Borderlands* and *Ratchet and Clank* that never quite found an audience to match the popularity of the games that inspired them.

The trend of turning video games into movies that started in the 1990s led to several hit-or-miss efforts. But it was not until 2001's *Lara Croft: Tomb Raider*, starring Angelina Jolie, became one of the biggest hits of the year that studios and movie stars realized that well-done adaptations could lead to big box office numbers. "'Lara Croft' brought the adventurous spirit of the gaming world to life on the silver screen,"[23] game designer and movie buff Alex Thomas told the *Toronto Star* in 2024.

In the years since, a *Tomb Raider* sequel and a reboot of the franchise were both big hits. And six movies based on the horror video game *Resident Evil* were all hugely successful. Other video game–based hits include *Warcraft*, *Pokémon Detective Pikachu*, *Rampage*, *Uncharted*, and *Five Nights at Freddy's*. Plenty of less successful adaptations had short, unprofitable releases, but the hits have attracted such big audiences around the world that studios have dozens of movies based on video games lined up for years to come.

The success of 2025's *A Minecraft Movie*, with a $150 million budget and stars including Jack Black and Jason Momoa, suggests that the massive population of gamers can pack theaters in the same way that comic book fans have turned out for *Iron Man* and the rest of the Marvel Cinematic Universe for years. "Video-game movies are overtaking superhero movies as the genre of choice," says Jeff Bock, senior box-office analyst for Exhibitor Relations. "These are the myths and stories that many generations gravitate toward. While gaming may not be as cool or as flashy [as film], if you make the right movie based on a game, this shows the people will come."[24]

> **"Video-game movies are overtaking superhero movies as the genre of choice."[24]**
>
> —Jeff Bock, senior box-office analyst for Exhibitor Relations

Many television adaptations of video games also have fared well. Shows such as *The Last of Us* and *Fallout* have many dedicated fans. However, *Fallout* star Ella Purnell acknowledged that adaptations can be tricky. "I think one of the big challenges about adapting a video game is you're changing the entire format," she told *Radio Times* in 2024. "You're going from a first-player experience, where you are playing the game and you're essentially creating a story within that world. You're taking away the major element that people play the games for, which is the ability to choose."[25]

While plenty of popular games have been made into films or television series, hit movies and shows have also been adapted into popular games. The entertainment website IGN, for example, reports that there are more than one hundred *Star Wars* video games. Some re-create stories from the films or feature popular franchise characters. Others are original games simply set in the *Star Wars* universe. Similarly, there are games based

Many television adaptations of video games also have fared well. Shows such as The Last of Us *(pictured) have many dedicated fans.*

on *The Matrix* and *Pirates of the Caribbean* movies as well as those featuring comic book superheroes, such as Batman and Spider-Man, and characters, like James Bond and Harry Potter, from popular literature.

In some cases, the video game version of the movie becomes more popular than the film it inspired. One example is *X-Men Origins: Wolverine*, which was less successful at the box office than other *X-Men* movies and was criticized for its plot holes and lackluster treatment of dynamic characters such as Deadpool and Gambit. However, the video game adaptation was a hit with many comic fans. "As it stands, the video game is remembered much more fondly than the movie,"[26] Dawson Nyffenegger wrote on the entertainment website Collider.

Sampling from Soundtracks

It is not just film and television producers who have enjoyed a profitable relationship with video games. Artists in other creative fields are drawing inspiration from the games they play.

Players who enjoy *Tetris* would probably recognize the theme song. The lively, unmistakable melody is a version of "Korobeiniki," a nineteenth-century Russian folk song, which is fitting because *Tetris* was developed by a Russian computer engineer in 1985. While *Tetris*'s designers introduced an old song to a modern audience, many video game makers are layering their games with new music that is often finding a life beyond the screen.

Tracks from games such as *League of Legends*, *Counter-Strike*, *Fortnite*, and *Dota 2* are so fun and recognizable that they are often played at sporting events (including non-esports competitions) to get the crowds hyped up. Many are remixed by DJs and played at dance clubs and parties. Likewise, musical artists sometimes sample bits of music, dialogue, and sound effects from games to place in their own songs. Skrillex, for example, borrows from *Legend of Zelda* in his song "Tears," and Thundercat samples the jump sound effect from *Sonic the Hedgehog* in his song "Special Stage."

"Crossing" Through COVID-19

Of the many coping mechanisms people used to get through the isolation of the COVID-19 pandemic, the simple, comforting game *Animal Crossing: New Horizons* emerged as a gentle winner. The game, in which a player controls a character who creates a home and community on an island populated by cute, chatty animals, became one of the best-selling online games during the pandemic. The timing of its release on Nintendo Switch coincided precisely with the beginning of mass lockdowns—March 2020. Quickly sensing that many people globally were turning to the game for comfort, escape, and a sense of community that eluded them in the outside world, the National Videogame Museum in England launched the Animal Crossing Diaries. The project allowed players to post entries of how they related to the game through their experiences in lockdown and dealing with the stress and uncertainty of the pandemic. "In the future, we'll be able to look at those and say that's representative of what the pandemic was like. But actually, I think that the Animal Crossing Diaries, as an archive of people's experiences, gives a fascinating insight into the psychology of that time," John O'Shea, creative director of the National Videogame Museum, told *The Guardian* in 2024.

Quoted in David Roskin, "'A Fascinating Insight into Pandemic Psychology': How *Animal Crossing* Gave Us an Escape," *The Guardian* (US edition), March 21, 2024. www.theguardian.com.

While many video game soundtracks are energetic, some include music that is more relaxing. Game creators use ambient music, which is usually gentle, instrumental music with no hard rhythm or beat, to accompany peaceful moments in a game narrative or to enhance a tranquil atmosphere. But rather than dismiss them as simple background tracks, many musicians have been inspired by these soundscapes.

Seattle recording artist Jake Muir, who performs under the name Monadh, says his career as an ambient music artist began when he took notice of the soundtracks of his favorite video games, particularly those in the *Final Fantasy* series. "I developed this love of video-game soundtracks, a lot of which is ambient but you wouldn't necessarily call it such,"[27] he told *Seattle Weekly*.

Beyond incorporating original music, some video game soundtracks feature classic rock songs, rap hits, or other tracks that are licensed by the artists or other rights owners. The *Grand Theft Auto* games and others, like *Tony Hawk's Pro Skater* and *Marvel's Guardians of the Galaxy,* have included classic songs

Many games have included classic songs from past decades. Grand Theft Auto *(pictured) features in-game radio stations that can be tuned to play music from the 1970s and 1980s.*

> "Spending hours immersed in a game's world often deeply connects players to specific tracks and can introduce new generations of gamers to songs they may have never otherwise known."[28]
>
> —Christopher Cruz, senior gaming editor at *Rolling Stone*

from past decades that many young gamers may never have heard before. The *Grand Theft Auto* series, for example, features in-game radio stations that can be tuned to play music. In *Grand Theft Auto: San Andreas*, the hit list includes James Brown's "The Payback" (1973), Rick James's "Cold Blooded" (1983), and Faith No More's "Midlife Crisis" (1992). In a *Rolling Stone* article ranking the best video game soundtracks of all time, writer Christopher Cruz suggests that people often get a little musical education as part of their game-playing experience. He wrote, "A truly great licensed soundtrack manages to weave itself throughout the entire experience in ways that make it essential to the gameplay. Spending hours immersed in a game's world often deeply connects players to specific tracks and can introduce new generations of gamers to songs they may have never otherwise known."[28]

Talk like a Gamer

While video game music has made its mark on pop culture, the language of video games has been almost as influential. Video game players also have their unique terminology, much of which has spread beyond the games themselves. For example, in a game, an NPC, or non-player character, is a relatively unimportant character that is controlled by the computer. In real life, gamers may refer insultingly to a random person they encounter as an NPC because the person seems to lack individuality and critical thinking.

Similarly, a person new to an activity or situation may be called a "n00b," which originated as a term for a newbie, or person inexperienced with a particular game. Other examples of gamer slang that is now a part of everyday language include *OP* ("overpowered"), which refers to going up against an excessively strong character in a game, as well as dealing with an overwhelming situation in real life. *Ragequit* can mean to leave a game in anger or frustration or do the same in other upsetting situations. *Boss* typically refers to

"Now we're in a whole new ball game of people having a shared cultural knowledge of video games, so we've started drawing on that as a way to express our reality."[29]

—Adam Aleksic, linguistics expert

a powerful enemy in a game, but it has become a term to describe anyone who exerts strength or authority.

One reason why video game slang is being heard outside of the gaming environment is because people growing up as gamers—even casual ones—find the words helpful in relating to others like them. "Now we're in a whole new ball game of people having a shared cultural knowledge of video games, so we've started drawing on that as a way to express our reality,"[29] says Harvard University–trained linguistics expert Adam Aleksic, who posts on Instagram as Etymology Nerd.

Dressing the Part

It is one thing to talk like a gamer, but it is something else to dress like one or even dress like a favorite video game character. These days, video games are influencing style and fashion, too.

Video games and characters can be found on T-shirts, baseball caps, hoodies, backpacks, and just about any other article of clothing or accessory. There are entire clothing lines dedicated to *Super Mario*, *The Legend of Zelda*, and other popular games. And in the world of cosplay (a blend of *costume* and *play*), where

The Revolution of Video Game Dance

Playing video games is usually thought of as a sedentary pastime. Most of the action is usually confined to fingers and thumbs on a controller. But video games have also inspired players to get up and dance, too. It all started in 1999, with the release of the pioneering game *Dance Dance Revolution*, or *DDR*. Players stand on a dance platform marked with colored arrows in a cross shape. A song begins and players receive cues for various dance steps. Their score is based on how well their footwork matches the music and the dance patterns on the screen in front of them. *DDR* has spawned many copycat dance and exercise games. *DDR* is also used in many schools as part of their physical education program and has become a competitive esport in many places. But it is not the only video game with a dance component. The dance moves of characters in *Fortnite* have also been adopted by gamers, with thousands of TikTok users showing their Floss and Rollie moves. Football players occasionally celebrate touchdowns with *Fortnite*'s Griddy dance, and popular singers often join in with their backup dancers to re-create moves very familiar to *Fortnite* players.

video game fans can go to great lengths to appear like their favorite characters, video games are directly influencing how individuals dress and act—even if it is more about performance than personal style. More than that, gamers are finding that the costumes and styles of their favorite characters are inspiring their own sense of self-expression, says fashion writer Afraz Adeel. In a 2023 article in *The Teen Magazine*, Adeel wrote:

> From the iconic fashion choices of video game characters to the bustling world of cosplay conventions, the influence of video games on style is undeniable. Gaming is not just about playing; it is about self-expression, and what we wear in these virtual realms often reflects our real-world fashion choices. The relationship between gaming and fashion goes beyond mere aesthetics; it dives into the realms of identity, community, and even commerce.[30]

Fashion is also becoming a feature of many games themselves. Players can place their characters or avatars in trendy or unusual outfits. Even high-fashion brands, such as Gucci and Louis Vuitton, have collaborated with game designers on exclusive in-game items. While players may not be able to afford these outfits in real life, they can at least dress their characters in virtual versions of the latest high-end fashions.

Pixels and Pop Culture

While video games once occupied a niche in pop culture confined to arcades or home consoles and computers, it is clear that they are a major force in shaping entertainment, fashion, and language. Journalist Elia Marquette predicts a long and influential role for video games in entertainment and popular taste. In an essay on the entertainment website Trill, she wrote, “Whether it’s through groundbreaking visual effects, emotionally resonant storytelling, or the passionate involvement of fans, video games are leveling up the world of entertainment in ways that will shape its future for generations to come.”[31]

CHAPTER FIVE

State of Play

"Numbers do not usually tell the whole story" is a popular phrase that suggests data does not capture the full context of a situation. However, with video games in particular, numbers say quite a bit. For example, an estimated 3.2 billion people worldwide play video games, according to the International Trade Administration. That is almost half the world's population. The global video game market in 2024 was worth more than $270 billion, according to Precedence Research, with an expected rise to $720 billion by 2034. By comparison, Gower Street Analytics reports that the global film box-office grosses were around $30 billion in 2024.

> **"Video games remain a mainstay in American households, as they have for decades."[32]**
>
> —Stanley Pierre-Louis, president and chief executive officer of the Entertainment Software Association

The future of video games is likely to be as colorful and exciting as their past. Advances in technology are improving the quality of games and the many devices they are played on. And while once video games were associated with the youth market, they are now enjoyed by everyone from toddlers to older adults. Those who grew up with video games tend to keep playing them into adulthood. The Entertainment Software Association (ESA) released a report in 2023 showing that 14 percent of all gamers are age fifty-five or older and that the average video game player in the United States is thirty-two years old and has been playing video games for twenty-one years. About one out of four players is under age eighteen. In announcing the report's highlights, Stanley Pierre-Louis, president and CEO of the ESA, said that video games have truly become an activity enjoyed by all generations: "Video games remain a mainstay in American households, as they have for decades. Playing video games has become the norm, as those who first learned to play on early consoles now share their joy of play with their own children and grandchildren, resulting in an expansive and diverse player community."[32]

Return of Computer Gaming

The rising popularity of PC-based games and the greater diversity among game players and developers is helping drive innovation in the industry. So, too, are changes in hardware and platforms. The very first video games were played on massive mainframe computers that could fill rooms in an institution, but these days the computers have gotten much smaller. Now a laptop PC can run popular titles like *Roblox*, an adventure and building game that boasts more than 380 million players a month, according to the news site MSN. A 2025 article on CNET notes that about 53 percent of non-mobile gaming sales belong to personal computer games, compared to 47 percent for home consoles. By

An estimated 3.2 billion people worldwide play video games. That includes men and women of all ages and ethnicities.

comparison, in 2005 the PC's share of the video game market was only around 29 percent.

PC-based video games have ridden a roller coaster of popularity through the years. When personal computers first started to become widely purchased in the early 1980s, consumers also began buying games to go with them. But when the Nintendo NES took off in the late 1980s and other consoles followed, PC gaming took a back seat to the slick home console systems and the rapidly growing set of games that went with them.

Nostalgia for old PC-based games may partially explain why they have rebounded in popularity, but other factors have contributed to the resurgence. Marketing platforms such as Steam and the Epic Games Store offer players a huge number of games, including older games and independently made games that are not available for consoles. Many newer computer operating systems feature backward compatibility, meaning they can play older games.

PCs also allow gamers greater customization of their gaming experience. PC users can tailor their hardware and software to their individual needs and preferences. Many newer PCs also feature better graphics than are available on home consoles and televisions. And perhaps most importantly, it is generally easier to play massively multiplayer online games (MMOGs) on a PC compared to a console. MMOGs are games that can accommodate many players (potentially millions), all playing simultaneously and interacting in the same virtual world. A type of MMOG called a massively multiplayer online role-playing game (MMORPG) is especially popular on a PC. Some of the most popular MMORPGs include *World of Warcraft*, *Final Fantasy XIV*, *Runescape*, and *The Elder Scrolls*. "MMORPGs are one genre that are lacking on consoles,"[33] says avid gamer Geno Rosario.

Whether they are developing new games for a PC or a home console, game creators and engineers look a little more diverse than they did in the first few decades of video game history. In its infancy in America, the video game industry was dominated by White males. Today more women, people of col-

Dealing with Video Game Bullies

Findings from a 2024 survey released by the Pew Research Center suggest that 80 percent of teens think harassment and bullying during online video game play is a problem, and 41 percent of the teens surveyed said they had been called an offensive name while playing. While there may be no way to stop video game bullying, there are some strategies to try when bullying becomes a problem. Experts with the US Department of Health and Human Services recommend reporting bullying or inappropriate behavior to the game group, team, platform, community, or game developer. When possible, try to block the bully from the game and unfriend them in social media and gaming communities. Taking a break from the game is also advisable. Victims may also get support and advice from a parent or trusted adult about how to handle harassing behavior.

or, and LGBTQ game developers are entering the field, bringing new perspectives and designing games that might attract more diverse audiences.

More Women Get in the Game

A 2022 study by Common Sense Media found that tween and teen boys spend about two and half times as much time playing video games as girls do. That same study found that 40 percent of boys play some type of video game daily, compared to 10 percent of girls who play video games every day. As a result, most video game characters are male, and the game situations—sports and combat—tend to reflect what society has deemed traditionally male interests.

Certain aspects of the gender gap are closing, however. The data-gathering company Statista reports that in 2006 only about one-third of video game players were female, but by 2025 almost half of all gamers were female.

But things are not changing as quickly behind the scenes. The 2024 State of the Game Industry report, an annual assessment of various aspects of the video game industry sponsored by the Gamers Development Conference, noted that men still make up two-thirds of professional game developers. That imbalance is at the heart of a longtime complaint about how female characters

> "If we want these games to look different, we need to have more kinds of people making them."[34]
>
> —Gita Jackson, video game journalist with the website Motherboard

are represented in video games. They are often victims in need of rescuing, supporting characters, or scantily clad characters who have little to do with accomplishing the main mission in the game. "If you look at who is making games, it's not at all a surprise," says Gita Jackson, a video game journalist with the website Motherboard. "If we want these games to look different, we need to have more kinds of people making them."[34]

Though changes are happening slowly, there are some signs that gaming's future will be more inclusive. The 2024 State of the Game Industry report found that while around 34 percent of game developers are female, that figure was only 25 percent in 2020. And in 2024 the video game news site Newzoo reported that an increasing number of new games are featuring women in

More women are gaming than ever. In 2006, only about one-third of video game players were female, but by 2025 almost half of all gamers were female.

leading roles and that sports game franchises are including more women's leagues among their titles.

Women in the video game industry say there is still a long way to go, but at least there is a greater awareness now of how the business can be more welcoming of women game developers and how female representation in games can be improved. "Inclusivity has taken big steps in recent years," says Julie Seifert, a talent scout with Kellen Interactive and an ambassador with the Women in Games program. "But we started from a pretty grim place with a lot of stereotypes against women who play games and women who make games."[35]

Game Design Education

The next generation of women game developers and everyone else in the industry are getting their start in ways that were not available at the dawn of the video game era. Today someone interested in a career in video game design can go to college to study just that.

Many of the earliest video games were designed by computer engineers, technology enthusiasts who happened to have an interest in gaming. While students could enroll in computer tech courses, there were few if any college curricula dedicated specifically to game design. These days, though, there are more than two hundred colleges and universities offering courses or undergraduate majors in video game design, programming, and art, according to the ESA. And video games have become an element within other college majors. Rich Taylor, the ESA's senior vice president for communication and industry affairs, said in an interview on the website Game Developer, "Today, video games are not only the fastest growing entertainment medium, they are also increasingly used in education and business for professional training and e-learning. These new college programs underscore the importance of the video games industry, which is well-poised to create additional employment and professional opportunities in the coming years."[36]

Since the early 1990s, the number of colleges offering degrees in video game–related fields has grown steadily. At the University of Florida, for example, students can earn a bachelor's degree and a master's degree in digital arts and sciences through the school's Digital Worlds Institute. Justin Marlin, the institute's assistant director of student services and administration, explains, "It's not just an art degree. It's not just a computer science degree or a communications degree. We are forcing students to think of all these things all at the same time. That is an emerging field and understanding someone who can think design-oriented, but also tech-oriented, as well. Games sit within that perfectly."[37]

No matter where the next wave of game designers learn their craft, they will be entering a rapidly changing industry seeking to enhance the game-playing experience in many ways.

Technological Innovation in Gaming

Throughout the history of video games, advances in technology and the creative minds of game designers pushed everything forward. Looking ahead, that same combination is already at work making games more fun, challenging, interesting, and different from the games that came before them.

Advances in artificial intelligence, augmented reality, and virtual reality (VR) are expanding how games look and how they can be played. Though VR is still a relatively new aspect of video gaming, it is already changing game design. Many early VR games were based on adventure stories, like tales from *Iron Man* comics and the *Star Wars* films, but newer games put players into competitive sports environments, like soccer, or scary situations, like haunted houses or zombie attacks.

"We're very much interested in how we can use the power of gameplay to really get people moving."[38]

—Cathy Craig, professor of movement at Ireland's Ulster University and VR game developer

VR is also changing online multiplayer games, giving players new ways to interact with their fellow competitors. And while VR action has mostly been limited to a headset and hand controllers, VR's future will soon include the feet. Cathy Craig, a professor of movement at Ireland's Ulster University and a VR game developer with INCISIV, says:

> We're looking forward to having feet controllers as well, because if you think about it that'll open up a lot more possibilities in terms of what you can and can't do. . . . We're very much interested in how we can use the power of gameplay to really get people moving, to really improve their performance as well. . . . We had a flavor of it when we had the Nintendo Wii back in the late 2000s.[38]

Virtual reality is changing online multiplayer games, giving players new ways to interact with their fellow competitors.

Video cards and graphics accelerators are also being updated to handle the speeds needed to deliver the new, more photorealistic environments of some games. Additionally, the core processors in gaming consoles and PCs are improving to manage the large files and gaming speeds necessary to run more resource-intensive games.

Game consoles themselves are undergoing continued modifications. Nintendo's Switch and Switch 2 are hybrid consoles that can be hooked up to home consoles for play or detached to be used as portable consoles. Similarly, the Steam Deck is essentially a handheld PC that can play PC games or be connected to a PC for streaming games or to transfer files. These unique variants will likely shape how gaming companies view the future of consoles.

Next Game

Predicting the future of video games has never been easy. Allan Alcorn, one of the developers of *Pong* back in the 1970s, was as surprised as anyone to see the prominent role video games have played in society. He said in an interview on the Atari Compendi-

Esports: Fun and Games and a Lot of Prize Money

Though competitive gaming really took off in the early 2000s, its roots go back to the early days of arcades. The first nationwide *Space Invaders* tournament was held in 1980. Ten thousand participants were vying for a $2,000 video game. During the next twenty years, similar tournaments were held for *Donkey Kong*, *Mortal Kombat*, and many other games. Interest in esports—the term used for competitive gaming—has only grown since then. Major League Gaming launched in 2002, becoming one of the top global organizations hosting video game competitions. The rise of esports has been helped tremendously by Twitch, the popular live-streaming platform that carries tournaments and other contests live to gamers worldwide. Esports Charts estimates that hundreds of thousands of tournaments—from small, local contests to massive international competitions—are held each year around the world.

What does that mean for serious gamers? The tech news site rAVe [PUBS] reports that total esports prize money in 2024 topped $1.7 billion. And for gamers interested in medals, not just money, the International Olympic Committee announced in 2025 that it would begin to host Olympic Esports Games in 2027.

um website, "I am happy to see how video games have become part of our culture. I never expected that to happen."[39]

Looking ahead, it is likely that video games will continue to primarily serve as entertainment, but games and their mechanics will also be used in education and other serious pursuits. In an essay for *Forbes*, Jared Thau, founder and CEO of Gameverse Interactive, envisions video games becoming much more than diversions and hobbies. He suggests games can play a role in bringing people together and solving challenges related to classroom learning, mental health care, physical therapy, and more. He writes, "If we embrace the potential of games to make the world a better place and build supportive institutions to help them do so, we can create a world where games help lead us toward a brighter future."[40]

SOURCE NOTES

Introduction: Level Up: The Rise of Video Games

1. Quoted in Sam Albuquerque, "Windermere High Hosts First In-Person High School Esports Tournament," *West Orange Times & Observer* (Winter Gardens, FL), May 3, 2024. www.orangeobserver.com.
2. Quoted in Entertainment Software Association, "Video Games Remain Lifelong Source of Entertainment for 190.6 Million Americans," May 16, 2024. www.theesa.com.
3. Quoted in Albuquerque, "Windermere High Hosts First In-Person High School Esports Tournament."

Chapter One: Press Start

4. Quoted in Matt Blitz, "The Unlikely Story of the First Video Game," *Popular Mechanics*, March 28, 2016. www.popularmechanics.com.
5. Quoted in Brookhaven National Laboratory, "The First Video Game?" www.bnl.gov.
6. Quoted in Ryan P. Smith, "How the First Popular Video Game Kicked Off Generations of Virtual Adventure," *Smithsonian*, December 13, 2018. www.smithsonianmag.com.
7. Quoted in Charles Russo, "'It Changed the World': 50 Years On, the Story of *Pong*'s Bay Area Origins," *SFGate*, March 10, 2023. www.sfgate.com.
8. Quoted in Russo, "'It Changed the World.'"
9. Quoted in GamesBeat, "How Tomohiro Nishikado Created *Space Invaders* 46 Years Ago—Exclusive Interview," September 24, 2024. https://gamesbeat.com.
10. Quoted in Jacopo Prisco, "*Pac-Man* at 40: The Eating Icon That Changed Gaming History," CNN, May 21, 2020. www.edition.cnn.com.
11. Quoted in ABC News, "The Death and Resurgence of Arcades in America," August 15, 2014. https://abcnews.go.com.

Chapter Two: Video Games Find a New Home

12. Quoted in Edward C. Baig, "*Pong*, the First Video Game with Mass Public Appeal, Turns 50," AARP, November 9, 2022. www.aarp.org.

13. Quoted in Keith Stuart, "Sega Genesis at 30: The Console That Made the Modern Games Industry," *The Guardian* (US edition), August 16, 2019. www.theguardian.com.
14. Quoted in Jeremy Parish, "Sega Genesis 25th Anniversary: The Rise and Fall of an All-Time Great," VG247, August 14, 2014. www.vg247.com.
15. Quoted in Matt Purslow, "How the PlayStation Changed Everything," IGN, December 4, 2024. www.ign.com.
16. Quoted in Michael Dobuski, "Xbox 20th Anniversary: Looking Back on Introduction of Gaming Console," ABC News, November 21, 2021. https://abcnews.go.com.

Chapter Three: Games in the Palm of Your Hand

17. Quoted in Glenn Derene, "Game Boy's Grandfather: Remembering the First Handheld Games," *Popular Mechanics*, October 1, 2013. www.popularmechanics.com.
18. Quoted in David Kindy, "Thirty Years Ago, Game Boy Changed the Way America Played Video Games," *Smithsonian*, July 29, 2019. www.smithsonianmag.com.
19. Quoted in Kindy, "Thirty Years Ago, Game Boy Changed the Way America Played Video Games."
20. Damien McFerran, "Retrospective: The Awkward Birth of the DS, Nintendo's Most Successful System," Nintendo Life, May 19, 2017. www.nintendolife.com.
21. Chris Lakewoods, "Mobile Game Development vs. Console Game Development: Key Differences," TechBullion, October 28, 2024. https://techbullion.com.
22. Sydney Butler, "Smartphones Were Supposed to Destroy Handheld Gaming, but It's Stronger than Ever," How-to Geek, June 7, 2025. www.howtogeek.com.

Chapter Four: More than Just a Game

23. Quoted in Ann Marie Chandy, "A Gaming Revolution: From Niche Industry to Pop Culture Phenomenon," *Toronto Star*, April 13, 2024. www.thestar.com.
24. Quoted in Chris Lee, "Video Games like Minecraft Are Replacing Superheroes as Hollywood's Dominant IP," *Vulture*, April 9, 2025. www.vulture.com.
25. Quoted in Tilly Pearce, "Fallout's Ella Purnell on How TV Show Beats Video Game Adaptation Fears," Radio Times, April 9, 2024. www.radiotimes.com.

26. Dawson Nyffenegger, "10 Movie-Licensed Video Games Better than the Movies," Collider, August 31, 2024. https://collider.com.
27. Quoted in Cate McGehee, "Sound Artist Jake Muir on Field Recording, Sampling, and Video Games," *Seattle (WA) Weekly*, January 18, 2017. www.seattleweekly.com.
28. Christopher Cruz, "The 25 Best Video Game Soundtracks of All Time," *Rolling Stone*, May 27, 2024. www.rollingstone.com.
29. Quoted in William Hunter, "Is Gen Z Talking About You Behind Your Back? Youngsters Have Started Using Video Game Terms Including 'NPC' and 'Sidequests' in Their Everyday Conversations—So, Do You Know What These Slang Words Mean?," *Daily Mail* (London), April 12, 2024. www.dailymail.co.uk.
30. Afraz Adeel, "How Video Games Are Shaping Fashion Trends," *Teen Magazine*, November 7, 2023. www.theteenmagazine.com.
31. Elia Marquette, "Leveling Up: How Video Games Are Changing the Future of TV and Film," Trill, September 13, 2024. www.trillmag.com.

Chapter Five: State of Play

32. Quoted in Entertainment Software Association, "Video Games Remain America's Favorite Pastime with More than 212 Million Americans Playing Regularly," July 10, 2023. www.theesa.com.
33. Geno Rosario, "PC Gaming vs Console Gaming," Puget Systems, September 15, 2020. www.pugetsystems.com.
34. Quoted in Sarah Karda, "Games Are for Girls: How the Industry Is Beginning to Close the Gender Gap," Texas Tech University College of Media & Communication, March 31, 2021. www.depts.ttu.edu.
35. Quoted in Paige Cook, "Celebrating International Women's Day: More Stories and Advice," *Pocket Gamer*, March 8, 2024. www.pocketgamer.biz.
36. Quoted in Danny Cowan, "ESA: Record Number of U.S. Universities Offer Game Design Courses," Game Developer, September 30, 2009. www.gamedeveloper.com.
37. Quoted in Chris Burt, "University of Florida Provides Real Career Paths Around Games," University Business, January 3, 2020. https://universitybusiness.com.
38. Quoted in Robbie Meredith, "Will VR and Movement Finally Dominate Gaming?," BBC, December 28, 2024. www.bbc.com.
39. Quoted in Brian Deuel, "Al Alcorn Interview," Atari Compendium, 2000. www.ataricompendium.com.
40. Jared Thau, "Gaming Beyond Entertainment: How Video Games Are Shaping the Future," *Forbes*, May 22, 2024. www.forbes.com.

FOR FURTHER RESEARCH

Books

Mike Diver, *Retro Gaming: A Byte-Sized History of Video Games—from Atari to Zelda*. LOM Art, 2023.

Nicolò Mulas Marcello, *Video Games: From* Pong *to the PS5*. Abbeville, 2024.

Jimmy Olsen, *The Ultimate Video Game Trivia Book: A Collection of Interesting Video Game History and Fun Facts for Gamers of All Ages*. Curious, 2024.

Jean Zeld, *The Age of Video Games: A Graphic History of Gaming from* Pong *to VR and Beyond*. Andrews McMeel, 2025.

Internet Sources

Lifewire, "Trailblazing Women in Video Gaming: Meet the Pioneers Who Shaped Design History," March 10, 2025. www.lifewire.com.

Polygon, "50 Years of Game History, as Told Through 60 Games," February 21, 2025. www.polygon.com.

Rolling Stone, "The 50 Greatest Video Games of All Time," January 6, 2025. www.rollingstone.com.

Screen Rant, "The History of PC Games: Everything We Know," November 28, 2022. www.screenrant.com.

Smithsonian Institution, "Video Game History," 2025. www.si.edu.

Websites

Entertainment Software Association (ESA)
www.theesa.com
The ESA supports the video game industry, including game developers and consumers. This site offers visitors a look at the history of video games, descriptions of the jobs involved in game development, behind-the-scenes stories about various games, and interesting research about the popularity of games around the world.

Game Developer
www.gamedeveloper.com
This news site covers video game releases, news about video game companies, and interviews with game developers. The site also offers

tips to aspiring game creators and features podcasts that cover everything from video game trends and a look at the future of the industry to conversations among gamers about their favorite video games.

RetroRGB

www.retrorgb.com

This website is exclusively dedicated to retro gaming. There are tips to repair or upgrade older video game consoles, news about game rereleases, a helpful glossary of technical terms related to console upgrades, and tips to get started in retro gaming. For anyone interested in learning more about classic consoles, this site is a good place to start.

Video Game History Foundation

https://gamehistory.org

This organization was formed in 2017 to collect information about the entire history of video games. Its website houses an extensive digital research library that includes original artwork by game designers, thousands of game-related magazines, and decades of game development materials. Access is entirely free.

Women in Games

www.womeningames.org

Women in Games is an international organization dedicated to getting more women into the creative and business aspects of games and esports. This site features interviews with women in those fields as well as articles for girls and women aspiring to enter the video game industry.

World Video Game Hall of Fame

www.museumofplay.org/exhibits/world-video-game-hall-of-fame

Housed at the Strong National Museum of Play in Rochester, New York, the World Video Game Hall of Fame recognizes the important developments in the history of video games. Its website archives photos and information about all the games that have been inducted into the hall, displays a timeline of video game history, and provides a chance for visitors to nominate their favorite games.

INDEX

PICTURE CREDITS

Cover: Shutterstock.com

4: Shutterstock.com
5: Shutterstock.com
7: Pryimak Anastasiia/Shutterstock
11: PitukTV/Shutterstock
14: INTERFOTO/Alamy Stock Photo
16: MOXCO Mateusz Sxymanski/Shutterstock
21: Pumpkinpie/Alamy Stock Photo
24: Girts Ragelis/Shutterstock
27: Vibbily/Alamy Stock Photo
29: Lightspruch/Shutterstock
33: Arthur_Shevtsov/Shutterstock
35: Matthew Corley/Shutterstock
38: TCD/Prod.DB/Alamy Stock Photo
40: Hamara/Shutterstock
42: Miguel Lagoa/Shutterstock
47: Chokniti-Studio/Shutterstock
50: PeopleImages/Shutterstock
53: Hananeko_Studio/Shutterstock

ABOUT THE AUTHOR

After graduating from the University of Oregon, James Roland became a newspaper reporter primarily focused on education. He later became a magazine writer and editor as well as an author of more than two dozen books. He and his wife, Heidi, have three children, Chris, Alexa, and Carson.